# The Nutrition-
# Fitness Link

# THE NUTRITION-FITNESS LINK

## HOW DIET CAN HELP YOUR BODY AND MIND

### BY CHARLES A. SALTER

THE MILLBROOK PRESS
BROOKFIELD, CONNECTICUT
A TEEN NUTRITION BOOK

I wish to acknowledge the support and assistance of my editor at The Millbrook Press, Mr. Frank Menchaca.

Library of Congress Cataloging-in-Publication Data

Salter, Charles A., 1947–
The nutrition-fitness link : how diet can help your body and mind / by Charles A. Salter.
p.    cm.—(A Teen nutrition book)
Includes bibliographical references and index.
Summary: Discusses food, diet, and nutrition as they pertain to general physical fitness and mental performance.
ISBN 1-56294-260-3 (lib. bdg.)
1. Teenagers—Nutrition.    2. Physical fitness—Nutritional aspects.   [1. Nutrition.   2. Physical fitness.]   I. Title.
II. Series.
RJ235.S35    1993
613.2—dc20        92-35146   CIP   AC

Published by The Millbrook Press
2 Old New Milford Road
Brookfield, Connecticut 06804

*This book is dedicated to
Dr. Luis deLerma and Dr. Carlota deLerma,
my wife's parents, and
Mr. Luis deLerma and Dr. Carmen Luz deLerma,
my wife's siblings, for
sharing their daughter/sister Carlota with me.*

# Contents

# The Nutrition-Fitness Link

*A Word of Caution:* This book discusses health, nutrition, and fitness in general terms that apply to most people. But each of us is also unique, with individual differences in bodily makeup that affect our responses to food chemicals such as nutrients and also to exercise. Not every medical finding applies in the same way to all teens. Before making any major change in diet or lifestyle, therefore, consult your physician about your own specific needs and limitations. As you get into a regular exercise or sports program, seek advice from a trained coach or other knowledgeable person who can help you gradually and safely develop an increasingly strenuous program.

# 1

## *Myths About Nutrition and Fitness*

You're nearing the end of your second lap in the season's most important one-mile race. All you hear are your spiked shoes chewing up the cinder track and your own labored breathing. Your heart feels ready to burst as you strain your legs to go faster . . . farther.

Four racers lag behind you; three have forged ahead. You're gaining slowly on Chatham, Central High's star miler. Can you hold this pace for two more laps? The late April heat squeezes the sweat out of you like water from a sponge. You're glad you had that extra water before the race this morning.

Chatham looks drier than you. His T-shirt is only slightly damp, and you remember him boasting about drinking nothing since last night to keep his weight down so he would be lighter on his feet.

You come around the first turn of the third lap and gain rapidly on him. Are you going faster or is he slowing down? Just before hitting the second turn, you snake around him and burst into the curve. The pounding of his feet fades away and you don't even look back.

Your eyes focus now on Smits, from Southside High, in second place. He's kept up a solid pace until that last turn, but now he's slowing down. The yards between you turn to feet, the feet to inches. He looks nauseous. You remember him bragging about carbohydrate loading last week. You shook your head then, knowing that was stupid for a race this short. This morning you saw him slurping honey for extra energy just before heading into the starting blocks. You were glad your coach had some nutritional smarts about such habits.

Smits struggles just inches ahead of you, a desperate look on his face. You pull up and start to pass, but he lurches to the right to block you. Agilely you dart left and zip ahead of him on the inside.

As you enter the last lap, only Coates of Northview High separates you from first place. You glance at the stands and see people getting to their feet, waving and cheering. Across the field you can see the finish line unravel. They're putting up the tape for the victor to burst through.

Coates sees the tape, too. You sense his confidence growing. But you know that competitive athletics requires mental as much as muscular strength. You're glad you had those brain-power snacks a few hours ago to help keep you sharp and alert to the end.

You're halfway down the last straightaway and kick the cinders to the side. Coates glances back at the noise, and his startled look tells all. For the first time he realizes how close you are. As his concentration breaks, you burst forward with all your might. The crowd goes wild. Screams fill the stadium and Coates turns panicky.

You concentrate on the track and hug the inside. You narrow the gap to ten feet, then five as you pull out of the last turn. You block out the crowd and the screams as you keep your eyes on that tape two hundred feet ahead of you.

You run all out and come abreast of him. Only a hundred feet left.

Desperation consumes Coates. He blows all he has left too soon.

It seems like hours that you both chug on . . . side by side.

Your teammates at the finish line jump and cheer.

The tape waits ten feet ahead.

You summon up all your power and charge ahead as Coates fades, gasping breathlessly.

You burst through the tape only inches ahead of him.

First place!

## The Nutrition-
## Fitness Link

This book can't promise you a win every time. But a crucial link exists between the kinds of foods you put into your body and the kinds of performance—both physical and mental—that you get out of them. This book explores that link, and it can help you if you:

- like athletics, whether you participate in team sports or work out on your own;
- want to keep your body healthy, looking and feeling good;
- want to keep your mind in tip-top shape and do your best in school;
- seek greater control over your moods and their changes, energy level, and sense of well-being.

Nutrition cannot provide all the answers for physical and mental fitness. Babe Ruth, though heavyset, was still a master of baseball. A broken leg will keep you out of a football game or off the ballet floor no matter how well you eat. A family crisis will dampen your mood or school performance in spite of your balanced diet.

Exploring nutrition scientifically, however, does provide some useful information. Unfortunately, this information is obscured by a great deal of misinformation that can harm your health and fitness, as in the case of the losing runners described at the beginning of this chapter. Well-intentioned coaches, parents, or others may provide advice based on rumors or wishful thinking rather than on scientific evidence. Let's examine some of today's fitness myths that hamper rather than help young athletes.

Myth #1: The more nutrients the better. Some trainers follow this motto. They preach the virtues of extra protein—a nutrient used to build muscle, other tissues, and hormones—and encourage consuming excessive amounts of protein foods, protein powders or drinks, or supplements of amino acids—the components of proteins. Other trainers push extra vitamins, minerals, or other nutrients. Scientific evidence shows that too much of any of these can be as harmful as too little. An overabundance of certain nutrients poisons the body or forces it to waste energy ridding itself of excesses. To maximize fitness and performance, you need the right amount of nutrients, but no more. A very active athlete may need more of certain nutrients than an inactive person. (See Chapter 2 for details.)

Myth #2: Special foods can enhance performance above normal. Many fitness consultants encourage the use of *ergogenic aids,* special food compounds said to boost energy and strength to give you a competitive edge. For example, some claim that bee pollen makes you run harder, faster, or longer. Scientific analysis, however, reveals that this mixture of plant nectars and pollens with bee saliva does not improve human performance. It can markedly hinder performance among those allergic to the pollen. A balanced, adequate diet will help you do your best. The few ergogenic aids that really can enhance performance do so by letting you exercise longer, but not by increasing speed or strength. (See Chapter 6 for more information.)

Myth #3: You have to eat muscle (meat) to make muscle. The muscles are composed largely of protein. To build muscle, athletes need to consume adequate amounts of protein and work out. Without special planning, however, the average teen gets more protein than is needed. Even a complete vegetarian can readily obtain all the required protein through a balance of plant foods such as beans, peas, nuts, and tofu. There is no need to eat special types of meat, specially prepared meat, or meat in large quantities. (See Chapter 2 for recommendations on daily protein intake.) Some meat does add pleasure and variety to the diet, but an excess should be avoided because it usually includes large amounts of saturated fat and cholesterol, both of which can contribute to heart disease later in life.

Myth #4: Athletes can safely eat all the fat they want because they burn it off. Athletes do burn far more calories than inactive persons. So they can eat more calories of any sort—fat, carbohydrate, protein—and still maintain body weight, provided they exercise enough. This does NOT mean, however, that a high-fat diet is safe or healthy for athletes. Excess animal fat (saturated fat) and cholesterol are associated with heart disease and other health problems whether one is physically active or not. Excess fat can also dampen athletic performance. So even the hardest-working athlete should also strive for a balanced, healthy diet. Watch out, therefore, for high-fat foods such as lunchmeat and other fatty meats, fried foods, whole milk and whole milk products, butter, margarine, salad dressings, and other products containing vegetable oils.

Myth #5: Eating sugary foods before an event provides extra energy. Since the body depends upon blood sugar, or glucose, for energy, it might seem that eating foods high in sugar before exercise will help keep the blood supplied with glucose. This practice, however, can have the opposite effect. Eating sugary foods can quickly *lower* blood sugar due to hormone influences. If you gulp a sugary beverage or snack just before settling into the starting blocks, your blood sugar will momentarily rise as the sugar enters your system. But your pancreas will quickly secrete insulin, a hormone that drives down blood sugar levels by forcing glucose into muscle cells or to the liver. A sugary food, therefore, may make you feel weak just when you most need energy. Avoid sweets for at least an hour before an event.

Myth #6: To get into a lower weight category, it's okay to fast or take water pills. This is a dangerous myth. Water pills are diuretics, which force the body to shed valuable water in excess urine. Fasting forces the body to burn its own reserves for energy. Both practices will take a few pounds off your scale weight. But both may seriously hamper your performance or even threaten your health. Peak performance requires adequate body water and ready energy. I know, for instance, an athlete who wrestled in high school and college. He regularly fasted and dehydrated himself to reach lower weight categories where the competition was supposedly easier. But he often found himself mentally disoriented during matches and fell far short of his ability at his normal weight. He would have been better off eating and drinking normally, then competing in his proper weight category while feeling his best. Dennis Tinerino, a Teenage Mr. America, has recommended that athletes carry bottled water and a plastic cup at all times in their gym bags.

Myth #7: Traditional carbohydrate loading is an easy and safe way to enhance endurance. There is a grain of truth to this. Your body can store only a small amount of carbohydrate, and you can quickly burn up all of it in a single event such as a marathon race. Planning a special schedule of low and high carbohydrate intake days over a period of time can "trick" your system into storing an extra load of carbohydrate for that big race. Such traditional carbo-loading plans have several drawbacks, however. They can lead to dehydration, unbalanced blood chemistry due to incomplete burning of fat, and hypoglycemia (low blood sugar)—all of which impair performance. Chapter 3 discusses a safer plan to achieve the same goal.

Myth #8: Food might affect the body but not the mind. Many sports enthusiasts recognize that nutrition plays a powerful role in athletic fitness and performance. But they ignore its effects on the mind. They assume that the mind is an independent "ghost" in the bodily machine, unaffected by the body's operations. In truth, the body and brain are interrelated. What affects one usually affects the other. Proper nutrition influences psychology, helping to control alertness, mood, judgment, and reaction time. A good diet helps harness not only your physical but also your mental powers for maximum achievement.

## Glucose and Glycogen

Getting information based on scientific evidence rather than myths is only the first step in understanding the nutrition-fitness link. Another step is understanding what kinds of energy sources the body uses.

We already saw in our discussion of Myth #5 that one of the body's key energy sources is *glucose*, or blood sugar. All forms of carbohydrate, from simple carbohydrates such as sucrose or table sugar to complex carbohydrates such as starch in fruits and grain products, can be broken down by the body into glucose.

Glucose is the simplest form of sugar. It moves freely through the blood, and the body uses it readily for energy. But the body can also store glucose, and in this form it is known as *glycogen*. Each molecule of glycogen consists of several linked molecules of glucose. The liver maintains the body's single largest store of glycogen, enough for about an hour and a half of continuous exercise. All muscles normally have a small but ready supply of glycogen. As the muscle supply declines during exercise, the liver releases more into the bloodstream, from which muscle cells draw what they need.

## Types of Exercise

The type of energy source that the body uses—and how the body uses it—depends on the kind of exercise in which it's engaged. Aerobic and anaerobic represent the two types of exercise the body performs.

• *Aerobic Exercise.* The word "aerobic" means requiring oxygen. To produce the energy required for aerobic exercise a person needs oxygen, which is breathed in from the air. With adequate oxygen, glucose can be fully metabolized, or put to use by the body, producing the maximum energy for exercise. When glucose runs low, body fat or protein can be used for energy, although these are not the preferred sources. Most forms of steady, long-term exercise—walking, running, swimming, bicycling, skating—that do not make the person breathless are aerobic.

• *Anaerobic Exercise.* The prefix "an-" means

without. Anaerobic exercise is conducted with insufficient oxygen. During anaerobic exercise the body metabolizes glucose for energy, but not fully. Each molecule of glucose produces far less energy than in aerobic activity, so muscle glycogen is depleted at a far more rapid rate. Anaerobic exercise produces increasing amounts of the partial glucose breakdown product lactic acid, which causes burning muscle pain and exhaustion, eventually interfering with further exercise. Exercise involving short bursts of intense or maximal activity—weight-lifting, short sprints—are generally anaerobic. Such levels of activity cannot continue very long.

Many activities combine both types of exercise. A distance runner, for instance, may begin with aerobic energy production but then finish the race at the fastest speed possible, shifting to anaerobic energy production at the end. The endurance phases of such sports as basketball, football, and soccer allow aerobic metabolism, while the maximal strength and speed phases become anaerobic. At the point of exercise intensity where you become breathless and can barely speak, you have shifted into anaerobic exercise.

Here's why the above distinctions are important. Anaerobic exercise requires glucose or its source, glycogen. Aerobic exercise, on the other hand, can also use body fat for fuel. In most teens, the supply of body fat is far larger than that of glycogen. Thus the normal teen athlete can engage in aerobic exercise for extended periods, but in anaerobic activity only briefly.

These distinctions should affect your choice of activity. If you want mainly to lose body fat, keep trim, and improve your heart, lungs, and overall health, then choose aerobic activities. If you want to build maximal strength or speed, then choose anaerobic ones, but only after you have developed good aerobic fitness to protect your heart from undue strain. In both cases, you should engage in regular exercise periods at least three times a week, for intervals of at least twenty to thirty minutes each time. For maximum performance both types of exercise require a healthy, balanced diet that avoids the extremes advocated by those who believe in the sports nutrition myths dismissed earlier in this chapter.

# 2

## Eating to Enhance Physical and Mental Fitness

All of us have seen pictures of the malnourished in the world's famine areas. With sunken eyes and bloated bellies they lie listlessly, unable even to brush flies off themselves. Fortunately, such malnutrition is rare among American teens. Even in this country, however, anorexics—those who starve themselves in the pursuit of extreme thinness—suffer severe, and often fatal, malnutrition.

At the other extreme stand the well-muscled, healthy, energetic individuals who carefully strive for the ideal nutritional balance. In between these two extremes fall most American teens. They are not starving, but the odds are they eat diets unbalanced enough to lead to one or more nutritional deficiencies.

## Common
## Nutritional Deficiencies

Let's discuss four deficiencies common among American teens. Each may seriously impair physical and/or mental performance.

• *Iron Deficiency, or Anemia.* The anemic teen has an insufficient supply of red blood cells, which carry oxygen to the muscles and all other living tissues. Lacking sufficient oxygen to expend normal amounts of energy, the anemic feels weak, unmotivated, and easily fatigued. The cause is usually a deficiency of iron in the diet, although a shortage of other key nutrients such as vitamin $B_{12}$ may cause anemia by interfering with the body's capacity to use iron. Blood loss may also cause anemia. For this reason, menstruating females should take special care to obtain proper amounts of dietary iron. Distance runners are particularly prone to anemia. Some sports-medicine theorists have even suggested that pounding the feet against hard surfaces thousands of times an hour actually squashes and destroys red blood cells. Surveys indicate that as many as one-third of female runners have distinctly low iron reserves, and probably most distance runners have at least marginal deficiencies of iron. Rich sources of this essential mineral include red meat and such vegetables as legumes (beans and peas), nuts, whole-grain items, and spinach and other leafy green vegetables.

• *Calcium Deficiency.* Calcium is the key mineral in bones and teeth. A severe shortage during development produces bones so weak that even standing and walking curves the legs outward causing bowleggedness. Such harsh deficiency, known as the disease rickets, would make competitive sports impossible. Milder inadequacies of calcium, though less visible, reduce skeletal and tooth strength. This makes bone breaks and tooth decay more likely. Low calcium intake over years causes problems in later life by aggravating osteoporosis, a condition marked by thin and brittle bones. The richest dietary sources of calcium are milk and milk products—cheese, yogurt, and ice cream. Legumes and green leafy vegetables such as salad greens and broccoli also provide calcium.

• *Vitamin A Deficiency.* A lack of vitamin A stunts growth, reduces disease immunity, and causes "night blindness" or difficulty seeing in dim light. Athletes with low vitamin A might find themselves more prone to colds, influenza, and other infections than better-nourished peers, although lack of vitamin A is not the only contributor to these infections. Rich dietary sources of vitamin A include liver, red/yellow vegetables such as carrots and squash, red/yellow fruits such as apricots and cantaloupe, green leafy vegetables such as spinach and turnip greens, fortified milk, and egg yolks.

- *Vitamin C Deficiency.* A severe lack of vitamin C causes the disease scurvy, symptoms of which include fatigue, joint pains, skin disorders, and swollen, bleeding gums. Such serious cases are rare in modern societies. However, even less severe deficiencies may also impair performance by reducing physical endurance, causing pains in the legs and joints, and robbing motivation. Rich sources of this vitamin abound. They include most vegetables, especially the green leafy ones such as kale, broccoli, and greens. Most fruits, particularly citrus fruits such as oranges, lemons, and grapefruit, also provide vitamin C.

## Deficiency Busting and Body Building

Did you notice how fresh vegetables supply many nutrients lacking in the American diet? Your mother was smarter than you realized when she said, "Eat your vegetables. They're good for you." Steve Reeves, the star of several *Hercules* and other films, had one of the most famous and muscular physiques in the history of Hollywood. And he was a partial vegetarian who ate mostly plant foods! Yet these foods are all but absent in the diet of many teens. They've been replaced by meat, sweets, and fatty junk foods such as potato chips.

Superb nutrition won't make you into a superhuman. It won't provide magical powers to help you excel in every sport. But it will help you reach your greatest potential as defined by your unique genetic makeup, medical background including diseases and accidents, motivation, and opportunity for training. If you have genes for small muscles, for instance, you will never become an Arnold Schwarzenegger no matter how carefully you eat. But a good diet along with exercise will make you stronger and healthier than a poor one will.

Good nutrition as you grow and train allows your body to build strong skeletal bones to support your weight in various physical activities. Good nutrition furnishes the raw materials for your body to build tough, agile muscles and connective tissues, provided that you work out regularly. And proper diet helps make your senses keen and your nervous system sharp, facilitating quick, decisive maneuvers on the playing field.

Given the choice, you wouldn't build your home with twigs and straw. You'd select the finest brick, mortar, and lumber. So provide your body the raw materials it needs to grow up strong and healthy—not junk but the best nutrients you can afford.

The following are some nutrition tips backed up by solid scientific information shown in the tables to help you build correctly your lifelong "home"—your body.

## Get Enough
## Food Energy

Your body runs on energy provided by the food you eat. We normally measure energy in terms of calories. The number of calories provided by each type of nutrient are found in Table 2.1.

### TABLE 2.1
### ENERGY PROVIDED BY NUTRIENTS

| Nutrient | Calories per Gram | Ounce (28.4 g) | Sample Food |
|----------|------|-------|-------------|
| Carbohydrate | 4 | 114 | 1 slice bread (12 g carbo) |
| Protein | 4 | 114 | 1 oz beef (7 g protein) |
| Alcohol | 7 | 199 | 1 beer (12 g alcohol) |
| Fat | 9 | 255 | 1 pat butter (4 g fat) |

Some distinctions, however, should be made. Pure protein and carbohydrate provide 114 calories per ounce. There are different types of carbohydrate, however, some better for you than others. Foods rich in complex carbohydrates include fruits, vegetables, and cereal grains such as breakfast cereal, bread, and pasta. These foods provide a stable, steady release of energy and also contain many valuable vitamins and minerals.

Simple carbohydrate foods such as sugar, regular soda, cookies, candies, and other desserts are usually considered "junk" foods. They supply energy, but in quick jolts followed by a rapid decline in blood sugar as the hormone insulin sweeps sugar from the bloodstream into the cells. Furthermore, junk foods provide little if any other nutritional value and may be high in fat. The diet of an athlete can tolerate some simple carbohydrates, but these should be minimized.

Protein can provide energy, but the body prefers to depend on carbohydrates for calories and put protein to work building muscles, hormones, enzymes, and other essential biochemicals.

Alcohol provides a great deal of energy, an excess of which is converted to fat, a fact to which many people with beer bellies can attest. Alcohol is not recommended as an energy source, however, especially for athletes. Alcohol depresses the central nervous system, interfering with balance and coordination, good judgment and planning. In large quantities it interferes directly with nutrient absorption, harms health, and shortens life.

Fat provides more calories by weight than any other nutrient. Not only are there visible streaks of fat in meat, but also invisible fat in each meat cell. Whole milk, whole milk products, nuts, and many snack foods, fried foods, and oily foods also contain fat. Butter, margarine, cooking oils, and regular salad dressings consist almost entirely of fat. Our bodies actually require a small amount of dietary fat, which does add flavor and enjoyment to food. But the average American teen eats far too much fat. Excessive animal fats are particularly dangerous, for they increase cholesterol levels. An overabundance of cholesterol over a lifetime clogs and hardens arteries, the vessels that carry blood to all parts of the body. As artery clogging worsens over time, heart attacks, strokes, failure of various vital organs, and even death may result.

Table 2.2 recommends how much of your total calories should come from each type of nutrient. Compare these recommendations to the actual average consumed by teens today: carbohydrate at less than 50 percent, protein at 15–20 percent, and fat at 40–50 percent. Even sedentary teens probably need more complex carbohydrates than they get. And athletes who work out strenuously need even more carbohydrates.

## TABLE 2.2
## RECOMMENDED
## DIETARY COMPOSITION

|  | Average Teen | Heavy Trainer |
|---|---|---|
| Carbohydrate | 55–60% of total calories (less than 10% as simple carb) | 60–70% |
| Protein | 10–12% of total calories | 12% |
| Fat | less than 30% of total | 18–28% |

What are some of the benefits of fulfilling these recommended requirements? Consider this. The average teen normally stores only about 2,000 calories of glycogen, the only form of reserve carbohydrate in the body. On a low-carbohydrate diet, this small supply declines progressively with each day of an active teen's training. In only a few days, glycogen stores drop so low that a teen simply can't keep exercising at his or her normal level. But one study[1] found that a diet consisting of 70 percent carbohydrate allowed young athletes to restore glycogen almost fully after each workout. This enabled them to continue a heavy training rate day after day. To keep up maximal activity levels over time, therefore, you must aim for about 70 percent of your diet to be in carbohydrates. In addition, complex carbohydrates facilitate glycogen formation more than do simple sugars, though both will suffice.

But don't increase your diet indiscriminately. Whatever the source of calories, consuming more than you burn will add to your store of bodily fat. Each pound of fat you lug around represents 3,500 calories of stored energy.

Table 2.3 reveals the average caloric needs of teenagers. Consuming about this much should allow you to maintain body weight. But keep in mind that these are only averages. Teens who are taller, heavier, have more muscle, or work out harder burn more energy and therefore require more calories to maintain body weight than others

TABLE 2.3
DAILY CALORIC NEEDS
OF TEENAGERS

|  | *Average* | *(Range)* |
|---|---|---|
| MALES | | |
| Ages 11–14 | 2,700 | (2,000 to 3,700) calories |
| 15–18 | 2,000 | (2,100 to 3,900) |
| FEMALES | | |
| Ages 11–14 | 2,200 | (1,500 to 3,000) |
| 15–18 | 2,100 | (1,200 to 3,000) |

their same sex and age. The ranges of calories (cited in parentheses) provide some indication of this variability for most teens. In each case the lower number represents the tenth percentile, and the higher number the ninetieth percentile, of energy intake based on national surveys of the U.S. population. But even these ranges don't include all teens. For instance, a fifteen-year-old male who is more active than 90 percent of his peers may need more than 3,900 calories just to maintain his current body weight.

Caloric intake is only one-half of the picture. Caloric use must stay in balance to maintain current body weight. In resting metabolism alone, the teen spends hundreds of calories a day maintaining the bodily processes required to sustain life—breathing, heart rate, nerve activity. Voluntary activities such as sports increase caloric use dramatically, as revealed in Table 2.4. These are average figures only. During a football game, for instance, there are moments of intense activity such as scrimmaging followed by times of inactivity such as crouching in a huddle. And some people put far more energy than others do into an activity such as dancing.

Maintaining your current weight depends on balancing caloric input with output. Some teens are lucky. They are so active physically that they can eat all the calories they want and not gain an ounce. If anything, they worry about how to eat enough food to keep their weight up. Some teens are not so lucky. Even though physically active, they must watch calories to keep from gaining excess weight. It all depends on your individual metabolism and body structure.

TABLE 2.4
AVERAGE CALORIES EXPENDED
IN VARIOUS ACTIVITIES

| Activity | Calories Expended Per Minute |
|---|---|
| Badminton | 2.8 |
| Playing pool | 3.0 |
| Horseback riding | 3.0 |
| Dancing | 4.0 |
| Ping-pong | 4.8 |
| Golfing | 5.5 |
| Tennis | 7.0 |
| Rowing | 8.0 |
| Bicycling | 8.0 |
| Bowling | 8.1 |
| Basketball | 8.6 |
| Football | 10.1 |
| Running (9 min/mile) | 11.4 |
| Swimming | 12.1 |
| Running (8 min/mile) | 12.6 |
| Running (7 min/mile) | 13.8 |

The size of your muscles depends on the genes you inherited from your parents, how actively you exercise those muscles on a regular basis, and your intake of dietary protein. Insufficient protein intake will prevent your muscles from building up. Excessive intake will not make your muscles larger or stronger, but rather will result in fat. Adequate amounts of protein will allow your muscles to strengthen to their maximum potential as limited by your genes and exercise regimen.

---

### TABLE 2.5
### DAILY PROTEIN REQUIREMENTS

| Sex | *Per Pound Body Weight* | |
| | *If Inactive* | *If Physically Active* |
|---|---|---|
| MALES | | |
| Ages 11–14 | 0.45 gram | 0.56 gram |
| 15–18 | 0.41 gram | 0.51 gram |
| 19+ | 0.36 gram | 0.45 gram |
| FEMALES | | |
| Ages 11–14 | 0.45 gram | 0.56 gram |
| 15–18 | 0.36 gram | 0.45 gram |
| 19+ | 0.36 gram | 0.45 gram |

---

Most American teens consume too much protein. (See Table 2.5 for teen requirements.) An average, inactive fifteen-year-old girl needs only about 0.36 gram of protein daily for each pound of body weight. If the girl weighs 110 pounds, the proper amount of protein equals 40 grams. One ounce of most types of meat provides about 7 grams (g), a slice of pre-packaged American cheese about 6 g, a slice of bread about 2 g, and a cup of milk about 8 g. Just one quarter-pound cheeseburger and glass of milk for lunch can provide this girl's protein need for an entire day.

Too much protein adds to excess calories, tends to dehydrate the body, promotes calcium loss, and causes overwork for the kidneys and liver in handling the load. It also can trigger gout—a painful inflammation of the joints—in susceptible individuals.

Young, growing athletes need more protein than inactive people, because exercise breaks down some muscle protein and slows new protein formation. This problem grows worse when the diet lacks sufficient carbohydrate, for then the body begins burning protein for fuel. Very active athletes may also lose some protein in their urine and sweat. Following a workout, the body builds the exercised muscle stronger than before, provided sufficient amino acids (components of protein) are available from the diet. The American

Dietetic Association recommends that endurance athletes increase their protein intake by 25 percent. (See the "Physically Active" column in Table 2.5.) Getting this much usually presents no problem, however, for practically all foods other than fruits contain appreciable protein.

Animal proteins, however, usually include large amounts of undesirable fat. Meat, poultry, and fish all contain considerable saturated fat—the worst kind—and cholesterol. Avoid eating more than one serving per day of fatty foods such as cheeseburgers. Try to obtain most of your protein from lean meat and plant sources such as legumes (peas and beans), other vegetables, and grain products. Do not rely on supplemental protein powders or beverages or on nutritional supplements composed of one or more specific amino acids. Such products are simply unnecessary since an average diet already contains more protein than needed. So why spend the extra money for a product that probably contains unbalanced protein? Claims that these supplements build muscle more effectively than ordinary dietary protein are untrue. Also untrue are claims that eating extra amino acids such as arginine and ornithine appreciably boosts growth hormone and muscle development. Regular exercise is the best way to raise growth hormone levels, whether or not you take these supplements.

## Get Sufficient
## Vitamins and Minerals

A lack of certain vitamins and minerals can impair performance or even cause specific deficiency diseases. Does the athlete need nutritional supplements to avoid such problems?

Not as a rule. A balanced diet with adequate protein sources and plenty of complex carbohydrates such as fruits, vegetables, and whole-grain foods should provide all the vitamins and minerals needed.

Some athletes get sold on the idea of nutrient megadoses. The RDA (Recommended Dietary Allowance) is the amount of a given nutrient that should adequately supply the needs of almost all normal individuals. A megadose is ten or more times the RDA amount. Some sports experts recommend intakes up to hundreds of times the RDA for certain nutrients. At such levels, the vitamins and minerals become more like drugs than nutrients. No one could consume such large quantities of them by eating ordinary foods. It might take a basketful of broccoli, for example, to equal a vitamin A megadose. I strongly recommend that you avoid all such megadosing unless it is prescribed by a licensed physician for a specific disease.

Megadoses can become overdoses. Excess of vitamins A, D, E, K, and $B_6$ are toxic. Excess intake of such minerals as iron can also lead to nutritional imbalances and other problems. Almost any nutrient taken in sustained megadoses has the potential to cause some unpleasant side effects. There's no evidence that megadosing improves performance among well-nourished teen athletes, so why take the risk? I once was consulted by a client who complained of increasing joint pain. He had to cut down exercise levels and needed massages daily to keep going. A look at his diet revealed that he took several vitamin A supplements daily, and sore joints are one sign of vitamin A toxicity. I recommended that he reduce his vitamin intake to normal. He did, and soon the joint pain disappeared.

If you have trouble balancing your diet—getting a mix of fruits, vegetables, and grains—or if you have developed a measurable nutrient deficiency, then one balanced multivitamin and mineral supplement per day should suffice for most teens.

## Get Plenty of Fluids

There's more water than any other single ingredient in your body. In newborns about 77 percent of total body weight is water. This proportion gradually decreases throughout childhood and the teen years. By young adulthood about 60 percent of a young man's total weight is water, while about 50 percent of a young woman's is. The average teen carries approximately 3 quarts of water in blood, about 9 or 10 quarts in the spaces between living cells, and an incredible 25 quarts within the billions of living cells.

Adequate amounts of water are essential to maintain all vital life functions. Water helps carry nutrients into and remove waste products from cells. It enters into numerous biochemical reactions, serves as a lubricant—try eating without saliva—and controls body temperature through evaporation of perspiration.

In hot weather you can lose up to a pint or two of water in perspiration per hour even when inactive. Fluid needs increase in dry climates and higher elevations, and as a result of caffeine consumption, which creates excess urine. And the demand for water becomes crucial during physical activity. Exercising strenuously on a hot day can cause you to lose four to eight pints—four to eight pounds—of water in just one hour! In an endurance event such as a long race or sports contest, you can become dangerously dehydrated.

Even if you can drink all you want throughout an event, you can still become dehydrated. The thirst drive is simply inadequate to maintain proper hydration. You can fully quench thirst after drinking as little as half the fluid lost in sweat, but all of it should be replaced. When working out,

**TABLE 2.6**
**SYMPTOMS OF DEHYDRATION**

| Percent body water lost | Symptoms |
|---|---|
| 1–5%<br>(1–6 lbs in a 120-lb teen) | flushed skin<br>loss of appetite<br>general discomfort |
| 5–10%<br>(7–12 lbs in a 120-lb teen) | headache<br>dizziness<br>difficulty speaking<br>difficulty walking |
| 11–20%<br>(13–24 lbs in a 120-lb teen) | shriveled skin<br>loss of urination<br>mental disorientation<br>loss of muscle control |
| above 20% | death |

especially in the heat, it is important to drink extra fluid before, during, and after an event. Drink more than you think you need to be safe. (The next chapter will discuss sports drinks that make this easier.)

Dehydration is no joke! The symptoms become progressively worse, as Table 2.6 indicates. When participating in sports, therefore, watch for such signs in yourself and others. Take prompt action when dehydration signs appear. Even a 2 percent reduction in body water can lower physical performance by 10–15 percent. Proper hydration may preserve not only health but also your competitive edge on the playing field.

## Plan a Sound Menu

At this point you may be wondering how best to put the information just discussed in this chapter to use in your daily life. How can you ensure that you get enough energy, complex carbohydrate, protein, vitamins, and minerals, and yet avoid too much fat and simple carbohydrate? This section puts it all together for you in a convenient and simple-to-follow formula.

No one likes to count calories or grams of food. Count food servings instead, and you'll ensure an adequate supply of all the nutrients you need. Table 2.7 provides the details. The first numbers apply to the sedentary teen. The second numbers indicate approximately how much a more athletic teenager may need to handle the increased demands of physical activity. Based on your own experience, hunger levels, and possible weight changes, adjust your intake accordingly. However, don't sacrifice one type of food so that you can eat more of another. Dietary balance, the spread of intake among the different food categories, is the important thing, because that ensures intake of the right mix of nutrients.

## TABLE 2.7
### RECOMMENDED SERVINGS PER DAY

| Food Type | For Less Active Teens | For Active Teens |
|---|---|---|
| Milk products | 3–4* servings | 3–4* servings |
| Meat & vegetable proteins (beans, nuts) | 2–3 servings | 3–4 servings |
| Fruits | 2–4 servings | 4–6 servings |
| Vegetables | 3–5 servings | 5–8 servings |
| Grain foods (bread, cereals, rice, pasta) | 6–11 servings | 10–18 servings |
| Sugar (candy, desserts) | 0–1 servings | 0–2 servings |
| Fats (butter, margarine, salad dressings) | little, if any | little, if any |

* Three servings of milk products are enough for most teens, but teenage girls who are pregnant or breast-feeding need four.

Serving sizes are normally one cup (8 ounces) for milk products, about 2 or 3 ounces for protein foods, and one cup for leafy vegetables or ½ cup for other veggies. For fruit, consider as one serving one whole apple (or similar size fruit), a wedge of cantaloupe or other melon, ½ cup berries, or ¾ cup juice. For grain foods count one slice of bread, one whole biscuit or roll, one ounce of cold cereal, and ½ cup cooked pasta or rice.

Memorize Table 2.7 or write it out on a small card and keep it handy. You'll find this an easy method for ensuring the proper nutritional balance. Whether you eat family meals at home, cook your own food, eat at the school cafeteria, or dine out at restaurants, you can always think in terms of the basic food groups and the number of servings of each you need. With a little practice, choosing the right foods can become automatic.

# 3

## Ideal Meals and Snacks Prior to Athletic Events

The last chapter provided guidelines for your regular diet throughout the year. But what should you eat in the days and hours just before a major sports event or athletic contest? Can what you eat, how much you eat, and when you eat affect your performance on the playing field?

In answering these questions, let's begin by exploring which foods you should definitely *not* eat.

### Foods to Avoid Prior to a Sports Event

Even if you consume the following foods throughout the rest of the year, try to avoid or minimize them in the final days or hours before a major event. They may dull your competitive edge.

- *Alcohol.* Alcohol dehydrates the body and clouds the mind. It can interfere with the liver's production of glucose, reducing your supply of ready energy. It will lessen performance.

- *Simple Sugars.* Minimize the candies, cakes, cookies, sugary sodas, and other sweets in the 24–48 hours before an event. As we have seen, a sugar load creates fluctuations in your blood sugar levels. Fill up on complex carbohydrates instead. If you really need something sweet, try ice cream or ice milk. Such dairy items promote a slower, more stable release of glucose than other sweets and even than some starchy foods such as bread and potatoes. (See Table 4.2 and Chapter 4 for an explanation.) These foods also contain many other valuable nutrients such as calcium.

- *Fats.* Most meals contain some fat. But in the final meal or two before an event, reduce fats, especially animal fats. Skip the big, juicy steaks. Hold the butter and margarine. Avoid fatty snacks such as potato or corn chips. Fat is the nutrient most slowly digested, keeping the stomach churning longer. This ties up blood in the digestive tract that you need in your arms and legs for best results during athletic performance.

- *Fiber.* Consuming food high in fiber or roughage regularly helps keep the gastrointestinal system in good shape. Minimize fiber during the final hours before an event, however, because fiber also slows digestion. It ties up water in the intestines that is needed elsewhere, and may cause an uncomfortable, bloated feeling, which slows performance. For that final meal before entering the stadium, minimize high-fiber foods such as whole-wheat items, vegetables, and fruits with heavy skins such as apples. Do catch up with your recommended servings of these nutritious foods after the game, however.

Now that you know which foods to avoid before an athletic event, which foods should you eat?

## Ideal Pre-Exercise Meals and Snacks

During short training bouts or events lasting less than an hour, your body will rely mainly on energy already stored as glycogen. But during longer events you will also use any food eaten shortly before the event. Plan to eat a small, high-complex carbohydrate meal or snack one to four hours before a lengthy activity. Experiment during practice periods to determine the best time gap for eating prior to the event and to find the right type and amount of food. Select light, easily digestible items such as the following.
   • *Fruit Juices.* Drink 100 percent natural fruit juices with no added sugar. Avoid punches, lemonade and other "-ades," and other drinks with

more artificial flavors or sweeteners than real juice. Real fruit juice contributes energy, vitamins, and very little bulk to your stomach.

• *Skim Milk*. Milk without the fat provides energy, fluid, protein, and calcium. The natural sugars it contains are released slowly into the system. Those with lactose intolerance, however, can't drink much milk. Their systems lack the enzyme lactase required to digest the lactose sugar in milk. Instead, the lactose they consume feeds the bacteria in their intestines, producing cramps, gas, and diarrhea. They can, however, buy over-the-counter pills or drops to add to milk, easing the effects of lactose intolerance.

• *Yogurt*. Dr. Susan M. Kleiner, nutrition consultant to the Cleveland Browns football and the Cleveland Cavaliers basketball teams, highly recommends yogurt for nearly all athletes. It is readily digestible, even among people with mild lactose intolerance who can't consume ordinary milk products. It provides energy and a generous helping of calcium, which is so important for strong, athletic bones. A teen should consume about 1,200 milligrams (mg) of calcium a day, and a single cup of yogurt can supply 300 to 350 mg. Try to avoid yogurt high in fat and sugar, however. Plain yogurt is ideal, but if you find it too bland, add a bit of fresh fruit juice, diet Jell-o mix, or a teaspoon of honey rather than eating highly sweet, fruit-flavored yogurt.

• *Bread.* Whole-wheat or other whole-grain bread is generally preferable to white bread because it contains more nutrients. It also contains more fiber, however. So for the pre-exercise meal, choose white bread. Don't add butter or margarine, due to the fat. But a bit of unsweetened, 100 percent fruit jelly or jam for flavor shouldn't hurt.

• *Pasta.* Spaghetti, macaroni, linguini, and other pastas are derived from grain, usually wheat. Like white bread, they are high in carbohydrate, low in fiber, and easily digestible. However, avoid adding lots of cheese and meat, both of which contain much fat. Add instead some tomato sauce with seasoning or just a sprinkle of grated cheese.

• *Liquid Meals.* Several liquid meal supplements on the market are aimed at athletes. These are not recommended for weight loss or as a regular replacement for meals. For occasional use as a snack before an event or to supplement normal meals, however, these may prove useful if you can afford them. They provide fluid and easily digestible energy and other nutrients without adding the bulk and the full feeling caused by fiber. Some liquid meal products have considerable amounts of sugars and other simple carbohydrates, and you'd be better off avoiding them. To eliminate that problem, you can make your own liquid meals, designing them to your own taste and budget. Just mix such items as skim milk, plain yogurt, fruit or pure fruit juice, and flavorings in a blender. And leave out the sugar and other sweeteners.

If you decide to sample the commercial products or home-made versions, don't wait until a big event to try them out. Always experiment during a practice session just in case you experience an unpleasant reaction such as nausea or weakness. If one liquid meal formulation bothers you, perhaps a different type wouldn't.

Another way to avoid complications is to understand the positive and negative sides of practices popular in the sports world: carbohydrate loading and consuming sports drinks.

## Carbohydrate Loading

As we have already seen, carbohydrate loading refers to the practice of "tricking" the body into conserving more than usual glycogen, the stored form of glucose in the liver and muscles. Remember that glucose is the primary fuel burned during exercise, and your entire bodily reserve is quite limited. For events shorter than 60 to 90 minutes, your normal glycogen supply should suffice, and "carbo-loading" serves no purpose. For longer events, such as a marathon race, you rapidly tire and slow down as your glycogen supply dwindles—sometimes called "hitting the wall"—

and your system switches to alternative sources of energy, that is, fatty acids and protein.

The aim of traditional carbo-loading is to postpone or avoid this depletion of glycogen. It works in the following way. The athlete works out heavily on days 6, 5, and 4 before an event. During this time, he or she eats a low-carbohydrate diet. This severely depletes the body's glycogen reserve and, in turn, triggers an alarm reaction in which the body tries to make all of the glycogen it can. On days 3, 2, and 1 before the event, the athlete rests and consumes a high-carbohydrate diet, providing the raw materials for the body to produce and store even more glycogen than usual. Thus, the athlete has "tricked" the body.

This regimen does boost glycogen. On the big day it allows the athlete to exercise longer before running short of this invaluable energy supply. However, traditional carbohydrate loading is NOT recommended for it has several drawbacks:

• Exercising heavily for three days on a low-carbohydrate diet reduces blood sugar, possibly causing weakness and distractibility.

• Restricting dietary carbohydrates raises blood acids, creating a condition called ketosis, which can cause nausea and dizziness.

• These blood changes combined may increase the risk of training injuries. If you push to keep exercising even when feeling weak, distracted, and dizzy, you may slip up. You could severely pull a muscle while lifting a weight improperly, fail to see a pothole and sprain an ankle while running, or mistime a jump in basketball and plow into another player.

• Dehydration may also result, reducing physical capacity (as explained in Table 2.6).

Danny Padilla, a U.S. Champion and World Champion body builder, described the typical reaction to a low-carbohydrate diet as "lack of energy for training, irritability, mood swings, lack of any sense of well-being, and awful cravings for sweets."[2] Can the athlete afford such reactions as this when preparing to compete?

To avoid these complications of traditional carbo-loading, an improved method of training and carbohydrate consumption has been developed. According to this method, the athlete exercises hard on day 6 before an event and moderately on days 5 and 4. It is important that this exercise be of the same type as during the upcoming event. During this time, he or she eats a diet moderate—but not low—in carbohydrates, aiming for about 50 percent of total calories in complex carbohydrates. On days 3 and 2 the athlete exercises lightly, and on day 1 rests. During this time, he or she eats a diet high in carbohydrates—about 70 percent of total calories. This revised regimen minimizes the discomforting side effects of traditional carbo-loading. Yet it just as effectively boosts glycogen levels and endurance.

As we saw earlier, carbo-loading serves no purpose at all in events shorter than 90 minutes, during which the normal supply of glycogen will suffice. During short events, in fact, a glycogen surplus will interfere with speed and agility because glycogen storage requires additional water. This excess water can add to body weight and create a stiff feeling in the muscles. Only as glycogen is burned up during a long event can this excess water, released into the system, help prevent dehydration.

## Sports Drinks

The thirst drive does not lead to adequate fluid intake during exercise. Some experts, therefore, recommend flavored sports drinks to encourage drinking. These beverages have the added benefits of providing additional energy and electrolytes to replace those lost in sweat. Electrolytes include ions—electrically charged atoms—such as sodium, chloride, potassium, and magnesium. The first two of these compose ordinary table salt, or sodium chloride. These ions are essential for nerve function, muscle contraction, and fluid balance in the bodily tissues. A severe shortage of sodium can cause problems in all these areas, leading to confusion, muscle cramps, and even coma.

A typical sports drink contains water, electrolytes such as sodium and potassium, and carbohydrate energy in the form of fructose, maltodextrin, or sucrose. If you decide to use a sports drink, experiment *before* an athletic event, during a heavy practice in which you engage in the type of activity you'll do during the event. Some athletes find sports drinks more a hindrance than a help. It's better to discover how they affect you prior to competition.

Before you decide to spend your hard-earned cash on sports drinks, weigh their pros and cons:

*The PRO side:*

• Because they have more taste than plain water, sports drinks may encourage additional fluid intake.

• Because of the sodium content, such drinks may rehydrate the body somewhat faster than pure water. Yet they don't quench thirst well, which encourages even more drinking.

• The added energy may help in long-term endurance events lasting over 90 minutes.

• Some athletes may get a psychological boost from sipping a brand-name sports drink.

*The CON side:*

• They cost more than plain water.

• They don't help during exercise periods less than about 90 minutes, during which glycogen will suffice for the properly nourished athlete.

• Some contain considerable amounts of simple sugars, which the athlete is better off avoiding during exercise.

• There may be no need to replace salts lost in sweat, for the average person consumes far too much sodium already. Probably only an unfit person working out in extreme heat or athletes in ultra-endurance events longer than marathons (for example, 50-mile runs) actually need replacement salts during the event.

• Most don't replace all the minerals lost in sweat, such as magnesium.

• They can be sources of added calories, posing a problem to teens trying to maintain or lose weight.

• In some teens, sports drinks containing fructose cause intestinal gas and discomfort.

A final caution on sports drinks: It is not recommended that you mix your own from raw materials unless you have adequate training in the chemistry of these drinks. Too much salt or the wrong kind of carbohydrate could hurt your athletic performance.

# 4

## Enhancing
## Mental Performance
## Through Food

Some teens care more for sports than for aca-
demics, while others care more about the letters on
their report cards than those on varsity sweaters.
Both camps often forget that the body and mind
are inextricably linked. What helps one often as-
sists the other; what hurts one often hinders the
other. The ancient Roman ideal of striving for a
sound mind in a sound body still makes sense
today, particularly in light of increasing scientific
understanding of how food influences mental performance and mood.

### Energy for
### the Brain

Your brain and body are connected most clearly in
their use of glucose as their primary source of

energy. As blood sugar begins to fall in the hours following your last meal or snack, your muscles and your mind feel fatigued and less vigorous. Your liver can release some stored glycogen to tide you over to the next meal, but its supply is very limited. Hunger intervenes to stimulate you to seek food. Eating a meal abundant in complex carbohydrates enriches the muscles and the brain with a vital supply of ready energy. This heightens alertness, stamina, and drive.

Lacking sufficient carbohydrate, the body can shift to burning fatty acids—released from the breakdown of body fat—for fuel. But the brain continues to rely on glucose. When glycogen supplies dwindle to a critical point, the liver begins to convert amino acids from protein into glucose to feed the brain. Unless you are unusually thin, you won't mind burning up fat deposits for muscle fuel.

But burning up protein for brain fuel is another matter. Since your body must rob its own protein stores to obtain amino acids—if none have recently been consumed—it breaks down its own muscle. This is the last thing an athlete needs—to destroy muscle to feed the brain. Every day, therefore, even when dieting to lose weight, remember to consume an adequate supply of complex carbohydrates to spare the protein in your own muscles from becoming a "meal" for your mind.

## Energy and Performance

Just as athletes often gobble up extra carbohydrate before a sporting event, scholars should make sure they get plenty of fuel before an intellectual event such as a test, study session, or term-paper writing marathon. Complex carbohydrates—foods such as fresh fruits, vegetables, and whole-grain products—will supply the brain the energy it needs to concentrate and work effectively. Simple carbohydrate snacks such as candy and soda may provide quick energy surges, but the drop in blood sugar that follows could harm performance.

## Brainpower Snacks

Be sure to chomp on plenty of complex carbohydrate snacks such as those in Table 4.1 before any intellectual event. The longer the event lasts or keeps you from food, the more important this practice becomes. When taking college board exams (which last about three hours), final exams (which last more than an hour), or when participating in intellectual competitions (such as debates or music recitals) in which you must wait your turn, eat even a bit more than you think you need. Just make sure you avoid items high in fat or sugar,

**TABLE 4.1**
**BRAINPOWER SNACKS**

| Fruits | Vegetables | Whole-grain items |
|--------|------------|-------------------|
| apple | broccoli florets | biscuit or roll |
| grapes | carrot sticks | English muffin |
| melon | cauliflower | "lite" popcorn |
| orange | celery sticks | pretzels |
| pear | tomato juice | whole-wheat toast |

which might blunt mental sharpness. For example, don't smother your toast or English muffin with butter and gobs of jelly. A bit of protein with your high-energy foods will also help you keep alert, as we shall see in a later section.

## Slow Energy Release Foods

The term *glycemic index* refers to the release rate of glucose into the system following ingestion of a carbohydrate food. The reference point is arbitrarily set for the glucose release rate of white bread at 100. The glucose release rate of other foods is then compared to this reference point. Foods with glycemic indexes higher than 100 produce a faster surge and fall in blood sugar, which usually drags down performance. Foods with numbers lower than 100 produce a slower, steadier release of energy without resulting in the sudden peaks and valleys in blood sugar levels. Foods with low glycemic indexes are ideal in the last meal or snack before a long mental event during which you won't be able to break away for a snack. In other words, they hold off hunger's weakness and distractibility longer. Table 4.2 includes several foods with very low glycemic indexes.

The numbers in Table 4.2 come from testing each food's effects on blood sugar separately. The possible effects resulting from mixing foods of high and low glycemic index are unclear. The average of the separate numbers of the foods eaten together might represent the effect of the total. But without further experiment we don't know for sure.

All of the foods in Table 4.2 may have a place in the diet. But consider those with low glycemic indexes when you want to feel mentally energetic and alert for a long period, especially if you won't have access to food or snacks during that time. Note that ice cream is the only dessert item with a low glycemic index. In general, teens eat too much dessert, and this book does not endorse an increase in consumption of desserts since nearly all of them contain considerable amounts of fat and sugar. However, the low glycemic index means that ice cream will give you a more sustained release of glucose than other desserts with similar calorie

## TABLE 4.2
## GLYCEMIC INDEX OF VARIOUS FOODS

| Low Glycemic Index Foods (slow energy release) | Glycemic Index |
|---|---|
| Soybeans (canned) | 20 |
| Cherries | 32 |
| Plum | 34 |
| Grapefruit | 36 |
| Peach | 40 |
| Red lentils | 43 |
| Skim milk | 46 |
| Pear | 47 |
| Chick-peas | 49 |
| Ice cream | 52 |
| Yogurt (plain) | 52 |
| Apple | 53 |
| Kidney beans | 54 |

| Standard Comparison Food | |
|---|---|
| White bread | 100 |

| High Glycemic Index Foods (rapid energy release) | |
|---|---|
| Instant potato | 116 |
| Cornflakes | 119 |
| Honey | 126 |
| Baked russet potato | 135 |
| Pure glucose | 138 |

(Adapted with permission from: Jenkins, D.J.A., et al., "The Glycaemic Response to Carbohydrate Foods." *Lancet*, 1984, vol. 2, p. 388.)

and fat content. Therefore, if you plan to eat dessert regardless of concerns over fat content, ice cream makes a superior choice for this reason.

## Nerves and Neurotransmitters

The brain communicates with all parts of the body through the nerves. Nerves communicate with each other via chemical messengers known as neurotransmitters ("neuro" for nerve and "transmitter" for communication signal). The ultimate source for these neurotransmitting chemicals is the diet, particularly protein. If you don't eat enough of the right nutrients, your brain may not be able to make as much neurotransmitter as it needs to function at its best for prolonged periods.

## Norepinephrine and Stress Resistance

One neurotransmitter important for enhancing mental ability is norepinephrine, also called noradrenaline. There is some evidence that this biochemical can boost stress resistance—keeping your mind sharp and alert when under pressure. Eating protein provides your brain with the amino acid—tyrosine—needed to make more nor-

## TABLE 4.3
## FOODS HIGH IN TYROSINE

(*Ranked in order of declining amount*)

Eggs
Skim milk
Brewer's yeast
Cheese (especially parmesan & cheddar)
Soybeans
Peanuts
Cottage cheese
Peas
Sunflower seeds
Beef
Wheat germ
Tuna

*Note:* The brain uses tyrosine to make norepinephrine. However, many of these tyrosine-rich foods, such as eggs and beef, are high in fat and saturated fat. Do not increase your intake of them. The vegetable and grain protein foods mentioned here also contain tyrosine and make healthier choices because they include less fat.

epinephrine. This theory is still relatively new, and we cannot claim it has been completely proven to help with all types of stress. Nevertheless, the dietary recommendation it implies—to eat adequate protein—is sound. You can always experiment on yourself and decide if you find protein helpful. Just make sure you get a reasonable portion of tyrosine in the meal before a challenging mental event such as a test or performance. (See Table 4.3.) But don't overdo your protein intake. As we saw earlier, protein should comprise no more than 10–12 percent of total calories. And avoid foods that are also high in fat or sugar.

If for some reason you can't get enough protein in a given meal, you might want to take a high protein snack an hour or two before a mental event. (See Table 4.4.) Just remember that it takes some time to digest a protein food and get the amino acids circulating in your bloodstream. Depending upon the amount and types of food, a good estimate would be two to four hours.

---

### TABLE 4.4
### SOME HIGH PROTEIN SNACKS

Chicken or turkey slices
Milk (preferably low fat or skim)
Soybeans and soybean products (such as tofu)
Cheese (preferably low fat)
Peanut butter
Hard-boiled egg

*Note:* These snacks are recommended only in small portions and for occasional use. Ingestion of protein servings as part of regular mealtimes is preferable.

---

At the beginning of this chapter, we saw the importance to the brain of sufficient complex carbohydrates. Table 4.1 included some good snacks for energizing your brain. At the end of this chapter, we saw the importance to the brain of protein, and Tables 4.3 and 4.4 listed some good food sources of protein. So two key nutrients that feed the body also feed the mind. The ideal meal or snack before a mental event will include both.

# 5

## The Food-Mood Connection

Sometimes events in the outside world influence our moods. We get a bad grade and feel depressed, or we win a contest and feel elated. Sometimes our physical condition affects our moods. We get a good night's sleep and feel zesty, or we catch the flu and feel like "death warmed over." Sometimes our own behavior directly affects our moods. For example, we feel guilty over hurting a friend, or ten feet tall after being kind to an old person needing help. In all these examples, we are probably conscious of what factors have influenced our moods.

Other times, however, we may experience mood swings that puzzle us. We have no idea what triggered them. Our circumstances may seem objectively rosy, yet we still feel apathetic and depressed. Severe, unexplained mood swings may require the assistance of a counselor or therapist. But what about the typically minor mood changes that affect all of us? Some of these mood alterations may be influenced by diet. While this does not imply that diet affects—or is even a major factor in—all moods, scientific research does show that many connections between food and mood do exist. Let's explore those connections.

## Malnutrition and Mood

Malnourished teens certainly experience some unhappy moods. Insufficient protein intake produces a weak feeling, while low blood sugar triggers not only painful hunger but also irritability. Finicky eaters and anorexics experience just such emotional changes. Even skipping a single meal may trigger an emotional outburst or flood of unpleasant feelings in some teens.

Such psychological shifts clearly interfere with social poise, mental sharpness, and physical prowess. Hoping to avoid impaired functioning, many teens follow often-heard advice to start the day with a solid, well-balanced breakfast. Starting the day in this way does make sense, but it may not be enough. Growing teens, especially those who are very active mentally or physically, may need periodic snacks as well as three "square" meals a day to keep their energy levels high and moods positive.

## Depression, Overeating, and Obesity

Whether a depressed mood is caused by school pressure, feelings of inferiority, or environmental stress, many people seek to relieve the mood through overeating, particularly simple carbohydrates. This leads to dietary imbalances and excessive caloric intake. Unless such a person also exercises vigorously, he or she will probably add additional pounds. Sudden weight gain itself depresses people. Some get into a vicious circle of depression, overeating, weight gain, more depression, and more overeating.

But not all overeating is "psychological" in this way. Sometimes it is a biological attempt to increase the supply of serotonin, which acts as a brain neurotransmitter and is associated with feeling calm and relaxed. Serotonin is a type of natural tranquilizer. Let's see how it works.

## Carbohydrates, Serotonin, and Sleepiness

Carbohydrate intake raises brain levels of serotonin in complex ways. Even though carbohydrate contains no tryptophan, the amino acid precursor of serotonin, consuming carbohydrate facilitates the entry of tryptophan from previous protein meals into the brain. The brain can use the extra tryptophan to manufacture more serotonin, producing such effects as increased relaxation and sleepiness.[3]

Although this theory is relatively new and has not been proven conclusively, some nutritionists say that a small snack of high carbohydrate, low protein food taken about an hour before bedtime should help you relax and fall asleep. (See Table 5.1.) You should not choose a food high in both nutrients, for even a moderate amount of protein can wipe out the carbohydrate effect. Caffeine

TABLE 5.1
SOME HIGH CARBOHYDRATE,
LOW PROTEIN FOODS

| Item | Portion Size | Protein Grams | Carbohydrate Grams | Calories |
|------|------|------|------|------|
| Banana[1] | 1 whole | 1 | 27 | 105 |
| Crackers | 4 whole | 1 | 9 | 50 |
| Orange juice[2] | 1 cup | 2 | 26 | 110 |

[1] Note: Almost any whole, fresh fruit has a similar profile. Avoid avocados, however, which are high in fat and also have more protein. Perhaps due to the presence of fiber, fruit produces a slower, more gradual effect than other carbohydrate foods.

[2] Any 100% real fruit juice will do.

from coffee, tea, soda, chocolate, and certain medications can also counter the carbohydrate effect.

Please note that the carbohydrate snack adds calories. If you are trying to maintain or lose weight, you might want to shift intake from another meal to this late-night snack. Because of the additional calories, some experts have recommended taking supplements of purified tryptophan instead. This book does NOT recommend such supplements, because they have occasionally caused serious, painful, and even fatal illness. Relying on natural, whole foods is far safer.

And please be careful not to make this procedure a habit or crutch. It will remain most effective if you use it sparingly—for example, the night before an exam or other special mental event. The carbohydrate technique is certainly preferable to sleeping pills, whether prescription or over-the-counter. All sleeping medications tend to leave you slightly groggy the next morning and not at your most acute mentally. But the carbohydrate technique merely increases the natural biochemicals that your brain is used to, so there's no lingering chemical effect the next day.

# 6

## Questions and Answers About Food and Fitness

Even though we've explored many aspects of the nutrition-fitness link, there are probably still some questions we haven't answered. Here are some of the more common questions asked of nutritionists.

### What About Ergogenic Aids Like . . .

*Bee pollen?* Many statements are made about the athletic benefits of bee pollen—that it provides rich protein, fights infection, slows aging, and enhances performance. Such speculation should always make one suspicious. Recall the claims of "snake oil salesmen" who boasted that their bottles of elixir could cure all ills. In actuality bee pollen does make a good food—for bees. They collect the pollen and nectar from flowers and bring it back to the hive, where the beekeeper has placed devices that collect it from their legs.

Bee pollen does contain protein, but far less than ordinary human foods such as soybeans. It often contains bacteria and fungi, and many people are allergic to it. There is no proof whatsoever that it improves human performance. Its primary appeal comes from the images it evokes of busy, fast-moving bees. Athletes wish they could move that fast for such long periods of time. But eating bee pollen will not make them buzz about like bees any more than eating bananas will make them as strong as gorillas. And it costs much more than most ordinary foods.

*Brewer's yeast?* This food supplement is filled with protein, B vitamins, and minerals. Its name suggests that it's better for making beer than muscles, but actually it makes a good nutritional supplement. It has no magical powers, however, and multivitamin pills combined with ordinary dietary protein can provide the same benefit.

*Caffeine?* Caffeine grows naturally in coffee beans, tea leaves, cola nuts (used in producing some soft drinks), and cacao beans (the source of chocolate). But make no mistake. Caffeine is a drug with distinct effects on the body. Caffeine stimulates the nervous system, but people vary in their sensitivity to it. A given dose of 200 milligrams (about two cups of coffee) will decrease fatigue, lower reaction time, and increase alertness in some people. In others the same dose may cause irritability, hyperactivity, headaches, insomnia, and tremors. In addition, studies done during the early 1990s showed that some people experienced withdrawal symptoms when they stopped using caffeine.

Some studies suggest that your system adapts quickly to caffeine, meaning that its performance-enhancing effects occur mostly during early use. After repeated use of even a few days or weeks, it doesn't enhance so much as allow you to regain your normal alertness. Some studies suggest that heavy use for many years may increase your chances of developing heart or pancreas problems.

On the positive side, caffeine can be beneficial if you are a long-distance runner by helping your body burn fat for energy sooner than usual. This spares glycogen, helping you to keep up your normal speed for a greater distance. Caffeine also allows you to exert yourself harder and longer.

Because of individual differences, however, some athletes find caffeine a help while others don't. In addition, most athletic associations allow only certain caffeine levels in the blood of competing athletes. Caffeine levels above 12 micrograms per milliliter of urine are banned as a type of doping—illegal drug treatments to enhance performance. This is roughly equivalent to drinking eight cups of coffee in a short period of time. Consuming this much caffeine, either in beverage or pill form, tends to dehydrate you because caffeine is a powerful diuretic. And dehydration impairs performance.

*Carnitine?* All muscles require carnitine, a substance that enables them to produce fat. There is absolutely no advantage in the athlete taking supplements of this, however. The body can produce all the carnitine it needs from lysine, a common amino acid found in almost all food proteins.

*Ginseng?* Some "health food" companies make extravagant claims for ginseng. It is supposed to be one of those mysterious secrets of the Orient that endow the user with special powers. Consumed as a powder, tea, or paste, it is said to enhance digestion, vitality, endurance, concentration, and ability. It is even said to protect the body from tissue damage. The reality is far different, however. Ginseng's source, the ginseng root, does contain stimulant compounds, as do many herbal plants. At best, ginseng probably does no more for you than caffeine from coffee or soda. And it is far more dangerous than caffeine. Negative side effects in some users have included elevated blood pressure, mental confusion, depression, and insomnia.

*Royal jelly?* This compound is produced by worker bees specifically to feed the queen bee. It does help the queen to grow larger than the other bees and lay vast numbers of eggs. Some claim that it can increase strength and athletic ability in humans. This expensive substance has an exotic aura due to its name and role in the insect world. But there is no scientific evidence that it provides any special advantage to human athletes. Those who claim otherwise are victims of wishful thinking or the "placebo effect." This is a medical term describing a situation in which sick people who believe a remedy will help them sometimes improve, even if the remedy is actually an inactive compound. Such improvement reflects the power of the mind rather than of the mixture.

*Sodium bicarbonate?* If you have an acid stomach, "bicarb" can neutralize it and make you feel better. How about "acid" blood? When you exercise without sufficient oxygen, lactic acid builds up in the blood. When the acid level reaches a certain critical point, eventually the muscles can't function any further. According to Dr. William Evans, a sports physiology consultant with the Boston Bruins hockey and the New England Patriots football teams, swallowing a couple of ounces of sodium bicarbonate can help neutralize this acidic tendency in the blood. That, in turn, allows the athlete to work out longer before reaching the point of muscle failure.

Some cautions should be noted, however:
- This will only help well-trained athletes who regularly engage in short-term anaerobic exercise (weight-lifting, for example). It won't increase endurance among joggers and others engaging in aerobic exercise, because they don't have the same buildup of lactic acid during exercise.
- It won't increase strength or the capacity to use oxygen.
- Too much sodium bicarbonate will cause nausea, diarrhea, gas, or even muscle cramps. How much is too much depends on individual differences and the amount of excess acid in the blood. Athletes who are aware of these limitations, however, may find that sodium bicarbonate is an effective ergogenic aid that allows them to work out longer at strenuous anaerobic activities.

*Spirulina?* This is another name for blue-green algae—the microscopic plants that grow in water—and is sold as a powder or in tablets. Like almost any plant food, spirulina is fairly high in vitamins and minerals. It is one of the few plant foods that include vitamin $B_{12}$, making it attractive to vegetarians. However, spirulina provides no special ergogenic powers to athletes. At best, it has no more nutritional power than an equal amount of salad. And because algae may pick up from the surrounding water various metallic elements, some of them toxic, spirulina is potentially dangerous. It is also expensive and not very tasty to most people. More conventional sources of vitamin $B_{12}$ include animal foods such as meat, eggs, and milk.

## Other Questions

*Do female athletes have special nutritional needs?* Yes, biological differences between the sexes do result in distinct nutritional needs for females who are very active physically. As we have seen already, menstrual blood loss can cause a deficiency of iron required for red blood cell production. Women are far more likely than men to run short of calcium and suffer an increased risk of osteoporosis.

Young women who exercise too much or grow too thin may suffer *athletic amenorrhea*. This means that their menstrual cycle stops because of all their athletic activity. Exactly how exercise triggers this problem is not clear, but it may be that extreme exertion reduces body fat below the level required to produce the sex hormones that control the menstrual cycle. Some seriously dedicated women athletes may prefer the loss of their cycle, but it is not healthy for reasons other than temporary sterility. Lowered levels of sexual hormones such as estrogen predispose these women to osteoporosis and bone fractures. Therefore, women with athletic amenorrhea should consult their physicians. Treatment usually includes calcium supplements, some reduction of exercise, and additional food intake. Severe cases may require medical treatments such as hormone therapy.

Pregnant women can remain physically active if their doctors permit them, though competitive sports are usually prohibited. The pregnant athlete should with her doctor select an individual exercise program that takes into account her changing shape and weight as the pregnancy progresses. For instance, she might try low-impact aerobic exercises. The fetus or unborn baby is not harmed by the pregnant woman's mild to moderate exercise, provided that she eats enough to cover the baby's nutritional needs as well as her own increased demands occasioned by the exercise. However, intense exercise such as during competitive events raises body temperature, and this is unhealthy for the fetus. Therefore, pregnant women should avoid intense exercise even when they feel capable of it.

*What if I have hypoglycemia?* Hypoglycemia means you have low blood sugar or glucose. The body depends upon a continuous supply of glucose in the blood. When glucose begins to drop in the blood of a normal person, the body responds by releasing glucose stores in the form of glycogen from the liver or by converting amino acids from protein into glucose.

The person with hypoglycemia, however, can't readily maintain normal glucose amounts, and the blood level continues to decline as glucose is used up. This causes such symptoms as dizziness, nervousness, and weakness. Such symptoms don't prove hypoglycemia, and can be associated with other causes such as hormone imbalance, liver disease, diabetes, or other organ problems that require medical treatment. Only a blood test can confirm hypoglycemia.

But true hypoglycemia can be very serious, indeed. If the glucose levels continue to decline, blurred vision, mental confusion, convulsions, and even coma can result. If you suspect that you have this problem, consult your physician at once.

There are several forms of hypoglycemia. In "reactive hypoglycemia," for instance, the person overreacts to certain kinds of food only. This form of the problem can usually be handled by careful diet and lifestyle changes. Avoiding simple sugars, eating complex carbohydrates and proteins, getting more fiber, and consuming several small snacks throughout the day—all these can help maintain normal levels of blood sugar. Exercise and weight control can help sustain bodily sensitivity to insulin, the hormone that helps regulate blood sugar levels. Having hypoglycemia does not necessarily prevent you from engaging in sports and other physical activities. However, athletes should not push themselves physically during an episode of low blood sugar. They should get a protein/complex carbohydrate snack and rest until the attack subsides.

*Does fat loading work?* Some people recommend this as an alternative to carbohydrate loading. Instead of eating a high carbohydrate diet prior to an athletic event, they recommend a very high fat diet for a two-week adaptation period. The fat-loading diet involves consuming as much as 85 percent of daily calories in the form of fat, with dietary carbohydrate hovering near zero. The remainder is protein. Even though these two loading plans are essentially opposites, the body surprisingly can adapt and perform about as well in both. That is, in the short run.

Fat loading is NOT recommended for several reasons:

- It contradicts all health warnings to lower fat intake. The average American consumes about 40–50 percent of daily calories as fat. The American Heart Association and other health organizations recommend reducing that figure to 30 percent at most. Less is even better.
- High fat diets are associated with a broad

spectrum of serious, life-threatening health problems such as clogging of the arteries, heart attacks, strokes, and cancer.

- A super-high fat diet lacks the rich supply of vitamins and minerals associated with a diet high in complex carbohydrates.
- While some dietary fat adds to food enjoyment, excess fat is not appetizing and difficult to digest. A bit of butter on toast is one thing, but would you enjoy eating gobs of plain butter?
- Exercise during a fat-loading diet quickly depletes glycogen. After that point, exercise is very unpleasant during the two-week period required for the body to adapt to burning fatty acids rather than glucose for fuel.
- The fact that both fat and carbohydrate loading "work" is of greater scientific than practical interest. There is simply no justification for trying a fat-loading diet when modified carbo-loading is healthier and more pleasant. (See Chapter 3.)

*Do any foods have steroid-like effects?* Anabolic steroids are illegal drugs that do help athletes build more muscle mass—provided they work out industriously while taking them. These drugs are terribly dangerous, however, upsetting the balance of sex hormones, causing liver problems, and seriously increasing the chances of death at a young age. They should never be taken for purely athletic reasons, but only when prescribed by physicians for specific medical problems.

Because steroid shots and pills are illegal and dangerous, some people have turned to foods that are claimed to have similar effects. Proponents teach that certain herbs, which are legally available, may contain similar hormones that will beef up muscle development in athletes. In truth, some herbs do contain compounds with hormone chemical structure and effects. However, these plant "hormones" are not anabolic or muscle-building. And the human body cannot convert these compounds into anabolic hormones after ingestion. Therefore, consuming these herbs has no effect on muscle-building or athletic prowess.

*Do extra vitamins make you stronger?* No. People with vitamin deficiencies may experience weakness and other problems that adequate nutrition can usually resolve or improve. But consuming more vitamins than are needed is not helpful and may be harmful. Excess intake of many vitamins is toxic.

*What if I crave the wrong food before an event?* If you decide to put the lessons learned from this book into practice, you will have very definite ideas about which foods you should eat before a physical or mental event. You will also know which foods to avoid at such times. But what if you suddenly develop a craving for the wrong food at just the wrong time?

Sometimes cravings come just from bad habits. But other times they may reflect genuine need. Your best bet is probably to eat more of the "right" food to dispel any further hunger. If the craving persists, promise yourself to get some of what you want right after the event. Even an authentic need should be able to wait that long. This requires discipline, but excellence in physical or mental fitness always does.

## Food, Fitness, and You

Simply knowing the path to physical and mental fitness does not guarantee that you'll follow that path closely. You must decide for what goals in life you are willing to make sacrifices. What few have realized until recently is that physical and mental fitness both require the same types of dietary improvements. This should double your motivation to improve your diet while striving for a sound mind in a sound body.

# Appendix A
## Source Notes

1. D. L. Costill and J. M. Miller. "Nutrition for Endurance Sport: Carbohydrate and Fluid Balance." *International Journal of Sports Medicine*, 1980, vol. 1, p. 2.

2. T. Kimber, et al. *Gold's Gym Nutrition Bible*. Chicago: Contemporary Books, 1986, p. 102.

3. E. Hartmann and D. Greenwald. "Tryptophan and Human Sleep: An Analysis of 43 Studies." In H. G. Schlossberger, W. Kochen, B. Linzen, and H. Steinhart (eds.), *Progress in Tryptophan and Serotonin Research*. New York: Walter de Gruyter, 1984, pp. 297–304.

# Appendix B
## Glossary of Terms

*Aerobic Exercise*—Steady, less-intense exercise in which breathing can keep up with oxygen need, allowing full burning of glucose with oxygen for energy.

*Amino Acid*—A component of a protein molecule. There are about twenty-two amino acids important in human nutrition, and these are arranged in long sequences to form protein molecules.

*Anaerobic Exercise*—Exercise in the absence of sufficient oxygen to fully metabolize glucose into energy. This occurs when exertion is so intense that even rapid breathing cannot supply enough oxygen.

*Diuretic*—A compound that promotes the loss of body water through the formation of additional urine.

*Ergogenic Aids*—"Ergo" means work and "genic" means producing. According to their name, these compounds are said to increase an athlete's work output. Few really do. Most help no more than ordinary nutrients, and some cause harm.

*Fatty Acid*—A component of a fat molecule. For instance, a triglyceride, which is a typical fat molecule, contains three fatty acids and a molecule of glycerol.

*Glucose*—This is the simplest molecular form of sugar. All dietary carbohydrates, including such complex ones as starch and simple ones such as sugars, can be broken down in digestion to glucose. This is the form in which energy circulates in the bloodstream—hence the alternate name "blood sugar"—to feed the body's cells.

*Glycogen*—The storage form of glucose in the liver and bodily muscles. Each molecule of glycogen is composed of molecules of glucose linked together.

*Hormone*—A biochemical messenger that is manufactured and secreted by a gland and then travels through the bloodstream to affect other parts of the body. Examples include growth hormone, sex hormones, and insulin.

*Insulin*—The hormone that helps regulate the supply of glucose in the blood. When carbohydrate is eaten and digested, blood glucose rises. Insulin is then secreted by the pancreas and rapidly drives the glucose level down to approximately standard levels. The excess glucose is driven into muscle cells and the liver, where some is converted to glycogen and the remainder is turned into fat and sent to the fat cells. This process is very important, because uncontrolled levels of glucose could lead to nausea, difficulty in breathing, intense thirst, and coma.

*Ketosis*—A condition of overly acidic blood caused by the incomplete metabolism of fat due to inadequate consumption of carbohydrate. The resulting nausea and dizziness may impair performance. Eating sufficient carbohydrate prevents this problem.

*Metabolism*—The sum of all the biochemical processes involved in breaking down food materials to produce usable nutrients or energy within the body.

*Neurotransmitter*—Any biochemical that transmits neural or nerve impulses from one neuron to another. Examples include norepinephrine and serotonin.

*Norepinephrine*—Also known as noradrenaline, this transmitter has several functions, including transmission of nerve signals in the areas of the brain dealing with alertness, concentration, and coping with stress.

*Serotonin*—A neurotransmitter that operates in brain areas helping to control relaxation, sleep, eating, and pain sensations.

*Tryptophan*—The amino acid that can be converted in the body into the neurotransmitter serotonin.

*Tyrosine*—The amino acid that can be converted in the body into several neurotransmitters, including epinephrine and norepinephrine.

# Appendix C
## Sports Organizations to Contact for More Information

Aerobic and Fitness Association of America
15250 Ventura Blvd., Suite 310
Sherman Oaks, California 91403

American College of Sports Medicine
P. O. Box 1440
Indianapolis, Indiana 46206

Gatorade Sports Science Institute
P. O. Box 9005
Chicago, Illinois 60604

Sports & Cardiovascular Nutritionists
Practice Group of American Dietetic Association
216 W. Jackson Blvd., Suite 700
Chicago, Illinois 60606

# Appendix D
## Further Reading

Brody, Jane. *Jane Brody's Nutrition Book*. New York: Bantam Books, 1982.

(This rather lengthy book provides an overview of many key research achievements in the nutrition field. It is written in a very approachable, chatty style, however. The interested teen could choose to read just the portions on topics of personal interest—for example, the caffeine controversy or the benefits of complex carbohydrates.)

Edelson, Edward. *Nutrition and the Brain*. New York: Chelsea House, 1988.

(This very readable book was written especially for teens. It explains in simple terms the complex scientific principles of the way that food affects the mind.)

Wurtman, Judith. *Managing Your Mind & Mood Through Food*. New York: Harper & Row, 1988.

(This is a very practical book with many examples of how food affects mental and emotional states.)

# *Index*

Sodium bicarbonate, 78–79
Soybeans, 66, 67
Spinach, 28, 29
Spirulina, 79–80
Sports drinks, 44, 56–58
Sports organizations, 91
Squash, 28
Steroids, 84–85
Stress resistance, 65–68
Sucrose, 22, 57
Sugar, 19–20, 22, 46, 49, 53
Sunflower seeds, 66

Tinerino, Dennis, 21
Tofu, 18, 67
Tooth decay, 28
Tryptophan, 71–73
Tuna, 66
Turnip greens, 29

Tyrosine, 65–67

Vegetable oils, 19
Vegetables, 27–29, 32, 40,
   41, 46, 50, 61, 62
Vegetarians, 18, 29
Vitamin A, 28–29, 41–42,
   42
Vitamin B12, 27, 79–80
Vitamin C, 29
Vitamins, 17, 32, 85

Water, 13, 42–44, 57, 58
Water pills, 20
Wheat germ, 66
Whole grains, 28, 41, 50, 52,
   61, 62

Yogurt, 28, 51